T0193177

Adoption?

Thank God for That Option!

Ana Monnar

To order additional copies of this book, contact:
Xlibris
844-714-8691
www.Xlibris.com
Orders@Xlibris.com

Book Designer: Jonah Goodman
Art Director: Mike Nardone

ISBN: Softcover   978-1-4010-8339-7
         Hardcover   978-1-4134-4143-7
         EBook   978-1-4771-8104-1

Library of Congress Control Number:2002095988

Print information available on the last page

Rev. date: 03/12/2021

This book is dedicated to my three loving children, Alberto, Anna and Alexander. All three were and forever will be a gift from God.

Foreword

Adoption is something to be proud of. Real parents are the set of parents or single parent that raises a child or children, not just gives an infant birth. There are an abundance of children that need a loving family, home, nurturing, good education, medical needs and anything else that should arise. Adopting a child is a big forever responsibility through good times and bad. You will love your adopted children equally as if you had given birth to them yourself. I've met many people that have adopted a single child and a very special loving couple that have adopted six children. I also met a couple that had two children of their own and later adopted a special needs child.

I am not claiming to be an expert in the topic of adoption. just speak from the heart and from personal experiences. It's up to each individual or pairs to make their own decisions. You can sense what is right for you and your family. Can and do you want to care for a sibling group, special needs child, infant, toddler or an older child? Only you know the answer to what you wish to do.

After the baby showers, portraits and all the family reunions come many other things. Remember that there will be more laundry, wear and tear of the house and cars, tutors if needed, selecting a good school, love, hugs, kisses, rewards, consequences, medical appointments, healthy meals, vacations, sports events, dance recitals and the list could go on. Just remember that the love and bond will always be there.

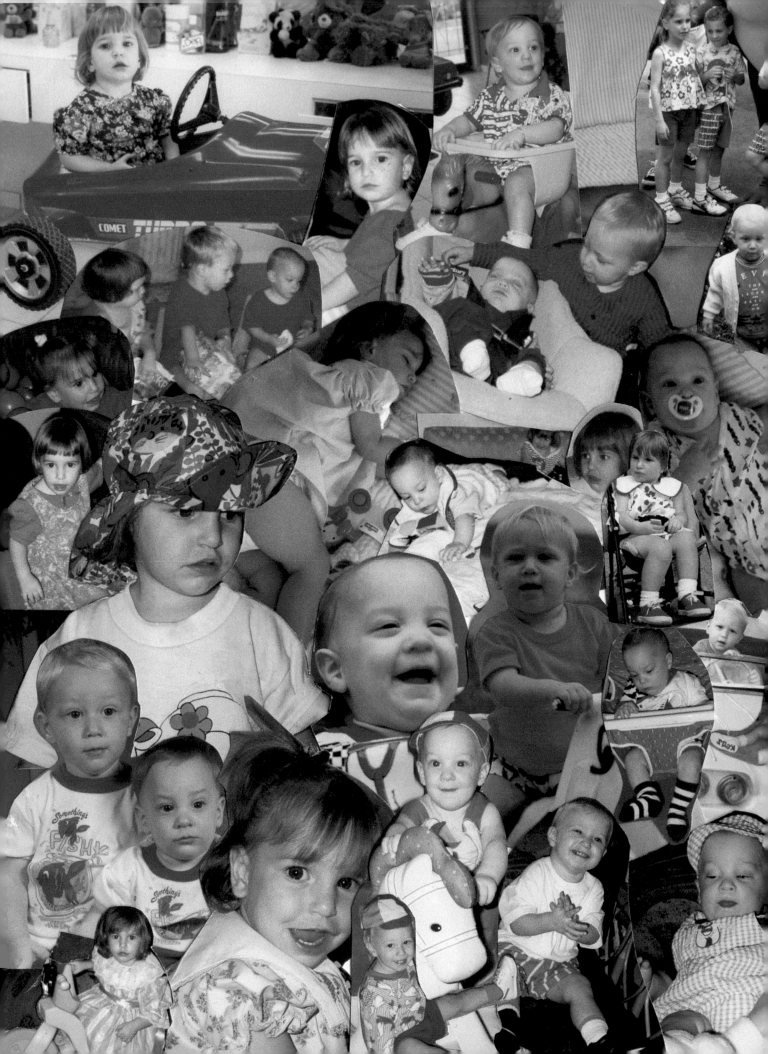

When did I tell our children they were adopted? They've known from day one with us. Even when they were too young to understand, I would very naturally say to each one, "God has blessed me with you. Thank God I adopted you." Not only did my husband and I adopt them, but they are also loved and accepted by their older sister Alina, their grandparents, aunts, uncles and cousins. We are all blessed to be a part of our three special and very loved children. I can't imagine what life would be without them.

Acknowledgments

I wish to express my gratitude to the
Department of Children and Families,
Judy Kreutzer, Guardian Ad Litem,
Dr. Walter Lambert,
Mary Lou Rodon-Alvarez,
The Guardian Ad Litem Program

I have three lively children.
As lively as can be.

Sometimes they test their limits,
rougher than the deep blue sea.

But no matter how good or naughty,
or how full the moon indisputably is.

Whether they act humble or haughty,
we love each other in our oasis.

My oldest son is special!
Special as can be!

He is noble, kind and giving.
His name is Alberto Lee.

Basketball is his favorite sport.

Faith, food, and sports
are his way of living.
Another good quality,
he is very forgiving.

My middle child is special!
Special in many ways!

She is a very loving daughter.

Loves many sports especially running, dancing and basketball.

Anna Lee has lovely grayish green eyes.
She is quite a leader.
She is also slim and tall.

My little one is special!
Special in precious ways!

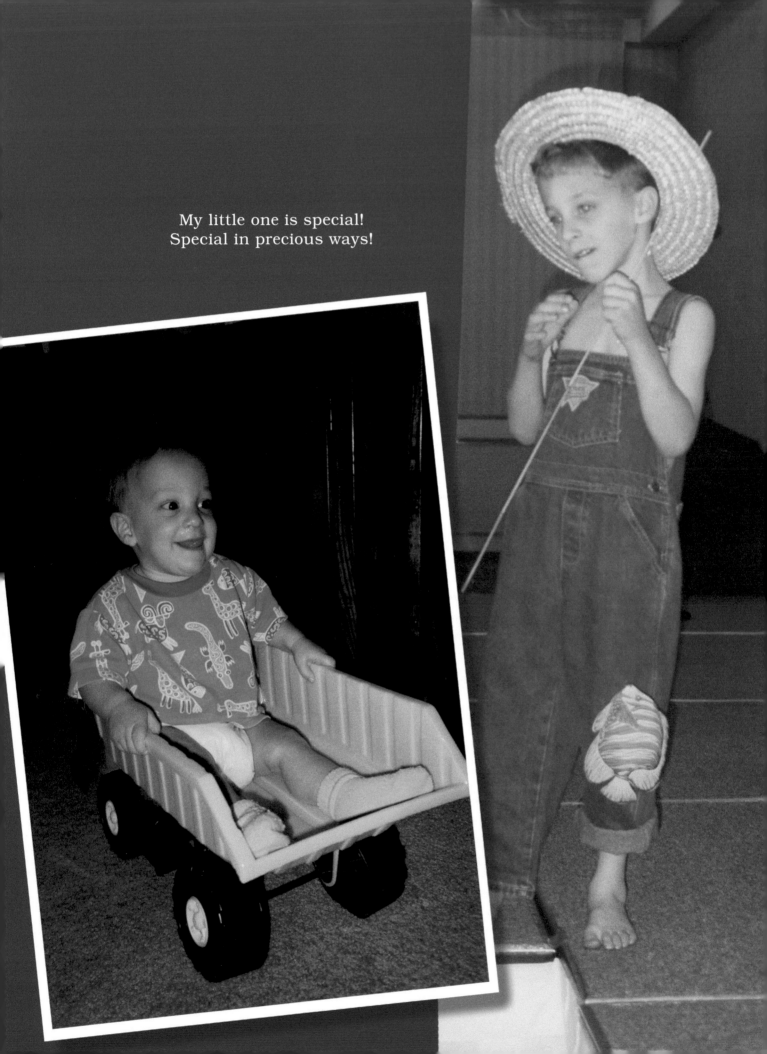

Alexander is quite an athlete.
He is also a fan of many sports.

His feet move very quickly.
He is very hard to beat.

He is also very funny, kind and sweet.

All three were a gift from heaven.
Thank you, God for blessing us.

With our three bundles of joy,
life is positively paradise and a plus.

The Gift

Give thanks to your
Biological mother
For giving you the gift of life
Sometimes for different reasons
Your birth mother
Cannot raise you
That's why God blessed
Adoptive mothers
With the gift of an adoptive child

It's quite a responsibility
To raise a human being
Important daily decisions arise
Preparing healthy foods
Offering care, safety and affection
Selecting a good school
To get a good education

No matter how good or bad it gets
For better or for worse
In sickness and health
I'm certain that not even for
Millions of dollars
Would an adoptive parent
Trade you in

Readers Are Leaders U.S.A., Inc.

www.ReadersAreLeadersUSA.net

Ana Monnar earned a Masters Degree in the area of Early Childhood and Elementary Education from Florida International University. Mrs. Monnar has been teaching for more than 20 years. She's taught second, third and fourth grades. She also had the opportunity to work as a Reading Curriculum Specialist and Reading Leader. She has written successful grant proposals and earned the title, "Teacher of the Year" in the 1980's. Mrs. Monnar has inspired many learners to write Award winning pieces. Her students have won trophies and certificates for District Contests such as Young Authors, Books With Wings and Poetry Contests.

Mrs. Monnar married Mr. Octavio Monnar on August 20, 1982. They were blessed with three children. Photography, reading, writing and going to the three children's activities are all fun and exciting diversions for the author. Mr. Monnar is currently suffering from Alzheimer's disease. He can't remember the names, but he can sense the love and bond is still there from his wife, children, family and close friends.

Printed in the United States
by Baker & Taylor Publisher Services